First Picture Dictionary
Animals
はじめての えじてん
どうぶつ

Pig
ぶた

Rabbit
うさぎ

Butterfly
ちょうちょ

Fox
きつね

Illustrated by Anna Ivanir

www.kidkiddos.com
Copyright ©2025 by KidKiddos Books Ltd.
support@kidkiddos.com

All rights reserved. No part of this book may be reproduced in any form or by any electronic or mechanical means, including information storage and retrieval systems, without written permission from the publisher, except in the case of a reviewer, who may quote brief passages embodied in critical articles or in a review.
First edition, 2025

Library and Archives Canada Cataloguing in Publication
First Picture Dictionary - Animals (English Japanese Bilingual edition)
ISBN: 978-1-83416-585-1 paperback
ISBN: 978-1-83416-586-8 hardcover
ISBN: 978-1-83416-584-4 eBook

Wild Animals
やせいの どうぶつ

Lion
らいおん

Tiger
とら

Giraffe
きりん

✦ *A giraffe is the tallest animal on land.*
✦ きりんは りくじょうで いちばん せのたかい どうぶつ です。

Elephant
ぞう

Monkey
さる

Wild Animals
やせいの どうぶつ

Hippopotamus
かば

Panda
ぱんだ

Fox
きつね

Rhino
さい

Deer
しか

Moose
へらじか

Wolf
おおかみ

Squirrel
りす

✦ A moose is a great swimmer and can dive underwater to eat plants!
✦ へらじかは およぐのが とくいで、みずの なかにも もぐって しょくぶつを たべます。

Koala
こあら

✦ A squirrel hides nuts for winter, but sometimes forgets where it put them!
✦ りすは ふゆのために どんぐりを かくしますが、どこにおいたか わすれることが あります。

Gorilla
ごりら

Pets
ぺっと

Canary
かなりあ

✦ *A frog can breathe through its skin as well as its lungs!*
✦ かえるは はだでも はいでも いきを することが できます。

Guinea Pig
もるもっと

Frog
かえる

Hamster
はむすたー

Goldfish
きんぎょ

Dog
いぬ

✦ *Some parrots can copy words and even laugh like a human!*

✦ おうむの なかには、ことばを まねたり、にんげんみたいに わらったり するものも います。

Cat
ねこ

Parrot
おうむ

Animals at the Farm
のうじょうの どうぶつ

Cow
うし

Chicken
にわとり

Duck
あひる

Sheep
ひつじ

Horse
うま

Pig
ぶた

Rabbit
うさぎ

Llama
らま

✦*A goat can climb steep rocks and even trees!*
✦やぎは けわしい いわばや きにも のぼることが できます。

Goat
やぎ

Peacock
くじゃく

Turkey
しちめんちょう

Mosquito
か

Dragonfly
とんぼ

◆ A dragonfly was one of the first insects on Earth, even before dinosaurs!
◆ とんぼは ちきゅうに さいしょに あらわれた むしの ひとつで、きょうりゅうよりも まえからいました。

Bee
はち

Butterfly
ちょうちょ

Ladybug
てんとうむし

Badger
あなぐま

Porcupine
やまあらし

Groundhog
まーもっと

> ✦ A lizard can grow a new tail if it loses one!
> ✦ とかげは しっぽが とれても あたらしく はえかわります。

Lizard
とかげ

Ant
あり

Small Animals
ちいさい どうぶつ

Chameleon
かめれおん

Spider
くも

✦ *An ostrich is the biggest bird, but it cannot fly!*
✦ だちょうは いちばん おおきな とりですが、とぶことが できません。

Bee
はち

✦ *A snail carries its home on its back and moves very slowly.*
✦ かたつむりは せなかに じぶんの いえを のせて、とても ゆっくり うごきます。

Snail
かたつむり

Mouse
ねずみ

Quiet Animals
しずかな どうぶつ

Ladybug
てんとうむし

Turtle
かめ

✦ *A turtle can live both on land and in water.*
✦ かめは りくでも みずの なか でも いきられます。

Fish
さかな

Lizard
とかげ

Nighttime Animals
よるに うごく どうぶつ

Firefly
ほたる

Badger
あなぐま

Kiwi Bird
きうい

Leopard
ひょう

Hedgehog
はりねずみ

Owl
ふくろう

Bat
こうもり

✦ A firefly glows at night to find other fireflies.
　✦ ほたるは よるに ひかって ほかの ほたるを さがします。

✦ An owl hunts at night and uses its hearing to find food!
　✦ ふくろうは よるに えものを さがし、みみで おとを ききわけます。

Raccoon
あらいぐま

Tarantula
たらんちゅら

Colorful Animals
いろとりどりの どうぶつ

A flamingo is pink
ふらみんごは
ぴんくいろ
です。

An owl is brown
ふくろうは
ちゃいろ です。

A swan is white
はくちょうは
しろいろ です。

An octopus is purple
たこは むらさきいろ
です。

A frog is green
かえるは
みどりいろ です。

✦ *A frog is green, so it can hide among the leaves.*
✦ かえるは みどりいろ なので、
はっぱの あいだに かくれる
ことが できます。

Animals and Their Babies
どうぶつの おやこ

Cow and Calf
うし と こうし

Cat and Kitten
ねこ と こねこ

✦ A chick talks to its mother even before it hatches.
✦ ひよこは たまごから かえるまえに、おかあさんと おしゃべり します。

Chicken and Chick
にわとり と ひよこ

Dog and Puppy
いぬ と こいぬ

Butterfly and Caterpillar
ちょうちょ と けむし

Sheep and Lamb
ひつじ と こひつじ

Horse and Foal
うま と こうま

Pig and Piglet
ぶた と こぶた

Goat and Kid
やぎ と こやぎ

www.ingramcontent.com/pod-product-compliance
Lightning Source LLC
LaVergne TN
LVHW072002060526
838200LV00010B/263